Surplus

Surplus

The Long Arm of Vietnam

Ed Gaydos

A companion to

Seven in a Jeep

A Memoir of the Vietnam War

www.SeveninaJeep.com

Columbus Press
P.O. Box 91028
Columbus, OH 43209
www.ColumbusPressBooks.com

Excerpt from *Seven in a Jeep* printed with permission.

Design by Brad Pauquette

Print ISBN 978-0-9891737-2-8

Printed in the United States of America
1 3 5 7 9 10 8 6 4 2

Contents

The Genuine Articles
An Excerpt from *Seven in a Jeep*

Kline came rushing into my hooch with an M16. He had been in FDC only a few months, but had already figured out the angles of life in the field. There was an eager look in his eyes that always made me nervous. "I'm sending this home."

"Kline, you can't send your rifle home. What if you need it for something, like shooting at the VC?"

"It's not mine."

"Then whose is it?"

"Nobody's."

"It belongs to somebody. The Army keeps track, you know."

"No, it's a combat loss. I filled out some paperwork after the last mortar attack and made it a combat loss."

"How'd you do that?"

"I got a form out of FDC. You weren't there. I wrote I was sitting on the shitter when the mortars started coming in, but I didn't say shitter, I said latrine. Then I said I jumped up so fast that my rifle fell down the hole. I wasn't about to go in there and get it, especially with an attack going on. The next day the shit—latrine waste I think I said—got burned, along with the rifle. See? A combat loss."

"Who signed it?"

"I just wrote the captain's name where it said OIC. That means officer in command, doesn't it?"

"No, but close enough."

"Anyway, I made it squiggly."

"You're going to jail."

"They gave me a new M16, so I've got this extra one that nobody knows about. Except now you and Junk."

"Well, you can't send it home."

"I think I can do it. I know guys that have."

"Kline, they X-ray everything that goes out of country."

"That's why I'm going to wrap it in tin foil, to fool the machine. Guys have done it."

"It's still going to look like a rifle."

"Not if I send it home one piece at a time."

"But even if you get it there, a fully automatic is illegal in the states."

"Really? Cool."

"What the hell, give it a try. I'll visit you in Leavenworth."

The next week Fred walked into my hooch. "I want to show you something," he said and handed me a photo album. "I'm gonna send this home to my folks."

"Wonderful," I said flipping through the pages, "I'm sure they'll like it."

"You didn't notice, did you?"

"Notice what?"

"The covers. Do you notice anything now?"

"They seem to be very nice covers."

"They don't look fat to you?"

"Well maybe a little, but nothing special."

"Yes," he said and pumped his fist.

"So what's the big deal about the covers?"

"They're stuffed with pot. And you can't tell, can you? Listen, this is the best weed in the world. You can't get stuff like this back in the world. And it's cheap."

"So your folks smoke pot. What is this, an anniversary present?"

When he grinned, his teeth stuck out in six different directions. "No, it's for me…for when I'm back in the world."

"You know if you get caught you'll go to jail."

"No I won't. It's foolproof."

"What the hell, give it a try."

What made me the go-to guy for sending illegal cargo through the U.S. Postal Service? Whatever it was I must have been good at it, because neither one of them got caught. To this day I imagine Kline in his den, a fire going, and mounted above the mantle is a fully automatic M16 rifle, the genuine article from Vietnam. And I picture Fred, seated in a circle of his closest pothead friends, the photo album on his lap, bragging about another genuine article from the war.

When the Military Police failed to show up for either Kline or Fred, I began to think about sending some of my own stuff home that I knew the Army would confiscate when I processed out of country. I had an AK47 banana clip, which I had come across partially sticking out of the ground on one of my jogs around the outside of our berm. Without thinking, I had bent down and pulled it out of the ground. It was only afterwards that it occurred to me what a stupid thing I had done. The VC, knowing the American weakness for souvenirs, often planted articles like this as booby traps. How many training films had I watched about booby traps?

I also had a handful of punji sticks, the sharpened bamboo spikes the VC planted in the ground along probable American patrol routes. I got them from a guy in one of the infantry units we supported. "They're all over the place out there," he said. "Smeared with shit ya' know, so you get infected when you step on one. But don't worry, I wiped these ones off."

I wrapped everything in tin foil and sent the package home to my younger brother Joe. When Joe got the package he was thrilled. A nosy teenager, he gave the banana clip a close look, and then took it apart. Inside, tangled in the spring, were five live rounds. I remember thinking that the clip felt a little heavy, but didn't give it much thought at the time. Then I realized that instead of a few wayward bullets stuck in its innards, the banana clip could have contained an explosive. What a present from Vietnam that would have made when young Joe opened the casing.

Today the bullets and the punji sticks are gone, lost in a move. The banana clip is back in my possession, a souvenir of the things that did not happen in Vietnam.

Seven in a Jeep is available from all major retailers,
and as an e-book on all digital markets.

www.SeveninaJeep.com

Forward

I originally wrote the following chapters for my friends and family, people who know me personally and might like to know how the story continues after my book, *Seven in a Jeep*, ends. In response to similar requests for additional material from reviewers and fans, I decided to release this section to the general public as well. These chapters reflect on how my time in Vietnam shaped me as a person, as a father and as a businessman. I hope you enjoy them.

Find out more about my memoir at
www.SeveninaJeep.com

THE REAL WORLD

March 1971

In Vietnam we called home the real world, a paradise where no one was trying to kill you. But after a while you got used to the mortar attacks, you settled into your sandbag bunker, you shot fire missions for the infantry because it was your regular job. You dreamed of home but it wasn't real anymore.

My first hint of home was the airline stewardesses on the Freedom Bird out of Cam Rahn airbase. I had forgotten what a female voice sounded like, and in the past year had spoken to an American girl for only a few minutes.

My first sight of home was from the window of the Freedom Bird circling over Tacoma. I had grown so used to brown sand and olive drab everywhere in Vietnam that the green lawns of the neighborhoods below looked fake, like they were put there by a movie director to impress the returning troops.

My first welcome to civilian life was on the campus of the University of Missouri. There I was an easy target for anti-war sentiment, and I was preached at by kids in bell bottom pants and manly beards.

None of it seemed real.

Goodbye

I was home just a few days and sitting on the couch when Mom walked through the room. On her way out she put a package on the coffee table. "This came in the mail for you."

It had a Department of the Army return address. I thought, *Maybe the Army is giving back my Darwin book.* Upon opening the package I was stunned and sat in dumb surprise. In my hands was a Bronze Star Medal. The date on the orders authorizing the medal was March 25, my last day in the Army and the day I flew home.

Mom came into the room again and said, "What was in your package?"

"It's a Bronze Star, Mom."

She said, on her way out again, "That's nice, dear."

Either Captain Joe or Top had put me in for the medal, and it felt like a goodbye handshake.

The medal came with a small service ribbon for wearing on the uniform, which I mounted on a charm bracelet for Kathleen.

Of the 2.7 million who served in Vietnam, just over 1% got the Bronze Star. Tim Coder also earned a Bronze Star, which he said, "They gave to everybody." Tim treasures above all his Infantry Combat Badge, awarded to infantrymen who come under live fire in a combat situation. He was happy to learn that the Bronze Star was not so widely awarded as he had thought.

Higher Education

Like a long vomit, I just wanted the Army to be over so I could move on with my life. A few weeks back from Vietnam, my skin fungus almost cured, I rushed into graduate school at the University of Missouri just in time for summer school. Gone were plans to bum around the country or take a boat to Bimini. I needed to get on with my life in a serious way. The main campus was in Columbia, a small town in the middle of the state. Downtown was right outside the campus gates and had one decent restaurant. The farms began a mile from downtown and did not stop until reaching Kansas City to the west and St. Louis to the east, 125 miles in either direction.

I had been dreaming for some time of living away from people and regaining my sense of personal privacy, and now I had the chance. For two years in the Army I ate, slept, showered, worked, played and sat on the latrine in public. Before that there were seven similar years in the seminary. In Vietnam I longed for the time when I could be alone. I wrote in a letter home:

I will need a few months by myself when I get home to work the regimented life out of my system. I think I am simply tired of people telling me what to do twenty-four hours a day. The desire for isolation is fairly common in the Army. Almost everyone I ask about their plans after the Army say they are going to live by themselves in the woods.

I rented a little place five miles east of town on a small lake, surrounded by pasture. The cows were perfect neighbors, they never gave orders and rarely carried guns. I had no telephone, figuring that if someone wanted to see me they could catch me outside class or drive out and knock on my door. It was heaven.

Life on campus was far from heavenly. I had hardly gotten the sand from between my teeth when I found myself in the charged environment of the college campus of 1971. Students were in a white lather over the war, with more passion than understanding. Loud and mindless, they reminded me of the cows bellowing outside my bedroom window.

"An unjust and unwinnable war." "Baby killers." "Post colonial imperialism," whatever that meant. And my personal favorite, "Make love not war."

When a few of my fellow graduate students found out I was just back from Vietnam they used me as their personal bayonet dummy. Young people who had never lived outside the covers of a book told me how I needed to think about Vietnam. They were passionate in their convictions, unencumbered by any real knowledge of Vietnam, and without life experiences to soften the hard edges of their opinions.

I always asked one question, hoping to find someone willing to be quiet for a second and listen, "Would you like to know what it was really like over there?" No one did. Had they taken the time to listen, they would have learned that I was not so much in favor of the war in theory, but very keen on fighting it in reality. My feelings were clear after just two weeks at LZ Sherry.

> The violent clashes on our college campuses over the expansion of the war into Cambodia is sad but understandable. I too would rather see an end to the mess, not a proliferation of it. However, we have allowed the enemy virtually unrestricted use of a "neutral" country for almost six years, while refusing our own troops the opportunity to cross the border. It's been a badly one-sided game. Infiltration routes run from Cambodia right through our backyard. And we pay for it in lives. When the mortars and rockets are making it hard for you to sleep, and you know where they're getting them

and you can't do a thing about it and a medevac flies out a dead or wounded nineteen-year-old – well you look at it differently than the well fed, scrubbed, secure college student.

The soldier in combat was simply not a topic of conversation on campus. His experiences did not have the sweep of ideology nor the grandeur of symbolism. The principles were more important than the people. That was the raw nub of it. The individual soldier was insignificant except as a foil for the politics of dissent. Fortunately I was still in an emotional dead zone, thinking to myself, *It don't mean nothin.* The anger and disappointment I came to feel about those early days on campus came later, the emotions waiting for their time.

The Hero's Welcome

Bob was a fellow graduate student, older and focused on his studies. I liked him because he spoke in a soft and measured manner. We talked about classes and professors, neither one of us volunteering much personal information. Bob walked with a limp and one day I asked him about it. He said, "I've got a prosthesis and I'm still adjusting to it."

"I never would have guessed." I decided to venture onto delicate ground. "What happened if you don't mind my asking?"

"Stepped on a mine."

"Wow. You loose it above or below the knee?"

"Above. That's why I'm having some problems."

We went quiet for a little while. Finally, I said, "I was in Vietnam too and just got back a couple months ago."

"Where were you?"

"Two Corps, outside Phan Thiet, at a 105 firebase."

He said, "Cushy artillery job, huh? I was up by the DMZ, around Quang Tri a lot. Nasty stuff up there."

"Yeah, anything near the borders. I had a buddy at Kontum. Same thing."

"I been back over a year, in and out of VA hospitals. Pretty depressing, all those guys with parts missing. Soon as I could get around on my own I got myself out. Now some days are good. A lot of them suck." Looking down at his legs, "So you couldn't tell, right?"

"No, all I noticed was the limp."

'Listen, I'd appreciate it if you wouldn't mention the Vietnam thing to anybody. They just don't understand."

"Yeah, I get it."

Thus was the hero welcomed home, shouted down and bullied into silence, a finger poked in the chest that held a Purple Heart.

My Madonna

Kathleen came to visit on weekends. She was working on a Master's degree in earth science, and turned our long walks in the woods into rock hunting expeditions. My job was to carry the rocks and load them into my VW bug, which groaned under their weight. She called the rocks her 100 million year old antiques. We took rides on my motorcycle, a little 175 Honda. Kathleen still carries a burn scar on her leg from brushing against the muffler. We loved to sit behind my country cottage contemplating the lake and watching the cows.

This was *my* hero's welcome. I thought I deserved thanks from a grateful nation and free drinks in the bars. Instead I got the welcome I needed: a dark Irish Madonna upon whose shoulder I rested my weary head.

In nine months we were engaged and a year after that we married. I don't know why she went out with me in the first place, or gathered me up after Vietnam. I had come back different somehow. Now at home in what I thought was the real world, I felt out of place, like a stranger just visiting for a few days.

I had lost the emotions that seemed to come so easily to others. I could only comment when others had tears in their eyes. When they laughed from the depths of their souls, I had to work to get up a smile. Nothing surprised or disgusted me. Most of all I could not feel compassion for the suffering of others. Their troubles seemed too trivial for all the bother. Vietnam had made me a cold observer, standing on the edge of life and looking in.

Kathleen said, "Give it time." And she was right. Over the months I traded my Vietnam neuroses for all my old ones, and probably a few extra. I returned to getting angry over details that did not matter and worrying about things that never came to pass.

One day I asked Kathleen about the plaid hip huggers that had enflamed my imagination when we first met. She said, "Oh, I threw those old things out a long time ago." I knew I had gotten over Vietnam when, upon hearing this, I cried like a baby.

Patton's Ghost

Four years later I was back at the University of Missouri in Columbia for a Ph.D. in industrial psychology. More graduate school reinforced my reputation with relatives as the perpetual student. Kathleen and I had been married for two years. I was still on the GI Bill and had a paid research assistantship.

Kathleen had to give up her teaching job in St. Louis and was looking for another teaching position in Columbia. She heard about an opening in earth science and math—she had a Master's in both—and managed to get an interview with the principal. She had never met the man, but learned he grew up in St. Louis. Before leaving St. Louis for the interview, we stopped at a White Castle and bought a dozen hamburgers. There were no White Castles in Columbia, and Kathleen was betting that the principal still had a passion for the smelly little things. You had to start on them as a kid to develop the taste, but never outgrew the love of them. She walked into the interview holding the bag behind her back. After the nice-to-meet-you's, she held the bag out to him and said, "I thought you might enjoy these."

"When she whipped the bag out," he said later, "I just

about fell off my chair. It was that wonderful aroma that got to me." The job interview went uphill from there.

Now with three sources of income and what we had saved, there was enough money to buy a new condo east of town.

I was a great runner in those days. My favorite place to run was the university golf course. The university track team held its long distance workouts there, and I blended in with the other moving bodies. There was nothing as wonderful as running on a golf course. This was in 1975 before golf hysteria gripped the nation. The course was relatively free of golfers, leaving the land free for its proper purpose: running through magnificent vistas, leaning around hills in easy strides and losing oneself in a great green cathedral.

When I did not have the time to drive to the university course, I would slip onto a private course just down the road from our condo. I waited till it was dark to avoid the complications of intruding on a private club. One night I drove to the course, parked my car on the lot under a lamppost as usual and headed into the night. As my eyes adjusted to the dark, the surrounding foliage emerged in shades of gray, here and there nicked with moonlight silver. I glided down the center of the fairways, the one moving object on a sleeping landscape. One night I returned to my car and leaned against the roof to do some light stretches, as I always did after a run.

A voice came out of the darkness, "Hold it right there."

I knew there was a gun behind the voice, there was not a doubt. I straightened up and turned to see a little guy holding a .357 magnum at arms length and pointed at my chest. The enormous pistol shook in his hand and sent wobbles through his body. By the light of the lamppost there was a wild, darting look in his eyes. I put my arms wide and said, "I was jogging. I

13

live just around the corner."

He looked at me for a moment and dropped the gun to his side, it still shaking in his hand. He said, "Oh, my God. I thought you were a burglar."

"I was just jogging."

"God I'm sorry. I thought...I didn't know. I thought you were..."

"It's OK. I should have told somebody I'd be out here."

He said, "You see they broke into the pro shop and got a lot of expensive stuff, clothes and shoes and clubs. I watch the place at night, it's all on me. I saw this shadow go by and I thought, *Not again goddamn it.* If I'd of known, but you see you coulda' been."

"You were just doing your job. It's OK."

"I coulda' killed you."

"But you didn't," I said. "Besides, I been shot at before. Forget it."

I turned and was almost to my car when he shouted after me. "I fixed your car so it couldn't drive off."

I turned back to him. "You what?"

"I pulled some wires off."

I went to my getaway vehicle, a 1968 VW Beetle originally red but now a fetching pink, and popped the rear hood. The wires to the distributor cap fanned out in all directions.

He was behind me now. "Want me to fix it?"

"No, I can do it."

"I'll hold the flashlight."

I said, "You do that." The pistol still dangled from his hand. "You know, you only had to pull out the middle wire. Not all five."

He said, "I don't know much about cars."

14

As I worked on seating the wires back where they belonged I said over my shoulder, "By the way, if I was the thief, what were you going to do with me?"

"I don't know. I just didn't want you to get away, you know, with the golf stuff."

"What if there were two of us and we both had guns?" No answer came.

Driving home I replayed the drama of having a small cannon pointed at me. When I saw the gun I felt like I was back in Vietnam, a detached observer doing what needed doing. In the car I should have experienced the aftershock of fear; I should have gotten a little shaky from the idea of lying dead in a pool of light from a lonely lamppost. But I felt nothing. Still today there is no emotion in the memory. It remains a mere catalog of events, not much different from how I remember the mortar attacks and fire missions at LZ Sherry. All the emotion of that night is centered instead on the violation of my car. A stranger's hands opened her rear bonnet and yanked her wires. I am still pissed about that.

The following week I saw the night watchman again. I held a minor office in our condo association and was attending a meeting of the owners and the developer. The condo board meetings were pitched battles over pets on leashes, illicit lawn signs and outsiders sneaking into the swimming pool. I would have traded these meetings in a minute for an honest NVA rocket attack. The watchman was at the meeting on a matter having to do with road access. After the meeting he pulled me aside. "Hey, you know I'm really sorry…"

"Nothing to be sorry for," I said.

"If my boss hears about this I'll lose my job." He nodded in the direction of a gentleman still in his seat and rifling through a stack of papers balanced on his stomach.

"There's nothing to hear about. Unless it's about how you fixed my car."

"Please," he said.

"Don't worry. It stays between us girls."

Walking back to my condo I thought of General George Patton, *Old Blood and Guts*. He died shortly after World War II in a jeep accident. Like him I could have been a warrior returned from battle only to be done in by a twist of fate, in my case shot by a watchman who pulled the trigger without knowing he was doing it.

Hired Killer

Fresh from graduate school I went to work for Anheuser-Busch at the corporate headquarters in St. Louis. A-B was in the early stage of rebuilding its human resources function when I walked in the door on a social visit. Before the interview was over the new department head offered me a job. I stayed for twenty-one years.

I was attending a conference in Phoenix and scanning the participant list when one name jumped off the page, William Beach. Could this be Captain Bill, my old gunnery instructor? I wove through the crowd at the cocktail hour looking at faces and scanning nametags. I saw him standing by himself with a drink in his hand. He looked beaten down and out of place in civilian clothes. There were little pads of fat under his eyes.

I said, "Captain Bill. I'm one of your students from Ft. Sill come back to haunt you."

His eyes dropped to my name tag before finding my face. "Oh yea. How you doing, Ed?"

"Well, I'm still here."

"Ft. Sill, huh? How long's it been?"

"Long. You were my ACL gunnery instructor."

"Yeah, that was a long time ago. Where'd you end up?"

"In 105s, direct support down around Phan Thiet."

"Remember anything I tried to teach you?" He looked at me sideways and I saw again the flint in his eyes.

"I never forgot about tube memory. I was going to be an FO, but it never worked out."

"I'm glad," he said, now turning serious.

"So Captain, what are you doing here?"

"Please, it's Bill. I'm a consultant, here scaring up business. Say, I have a suite. Why don't you come on up."

In his room he pulled a traveling flask from a briefcase and said, "You drink scotch?"

"Not so much anymore, Captain," I said.

"You keep that captain crap up and I'll kick your butt— again." He poured into the fancy cap. "To your health. So Ed, what kind of business are you in these days?"

"Beer. I work for Anheuser-Busch."

"I do strategy consulting. You name it, marketing, sales, brand work, if there's a buck I do it."

"Captain, why did you leave the Army for God's sake?"

"Same reason you left, my friend."

"But you were perfect for…" I could not find the right word, so took another tack. "Do you remember when you said in class you could always be a paper hanger, and somebody said, 'Or a hired killer?'"

"Yeah, that I remember." He paused. "But I already was, and that's why I got out."

18

Poof

I sat on the side of a hill at our church athletic field watching my young daughter Elizabeth play soccer. A horde of little girls chased the ball, twenty-two legs flying with lethal intent and putting up a cloud of dust. A young man with short hair sat near me. I overheard a part of his conversation that made me slide over and say, "You artillery?"

He said, "Yeah, just got out of gunnery school."

"Ft. Sill?"

"Yeah."

I said, "What piece did you train on?"

"155s."

"Me too," I said, "but a long time ago. I'm curious, did you get any forward observer training?"

"For sure."

"And how does that work these days?" I was ready to hear about the FO equipped with a map, a compass, a twenty-six pound radio on his back, spare batteries, flares, smoke grenades, two good eyes and two brass balls.

He said, "It's awesome, man. I mean, sir. We have this

19

laser gun we point at the target. The data goes up to a satellite and then down to fire control where it all gets computed for the guns. Then *poof*, no more target."

And *poof*, I was old.

Pilgrimage

Years later on a driving vacation with Kathleen and our daughters Elizabeth and Ellen, I insisted we take a detour to Ft. Sill. It was my first trip back. The buildings I remembered so vividly were gone, replaced by sleek, multistory piles of red brick. I drove aimlessly around the base looking for anything familiar. Then I turned a corner and drove into 1969. There was my old AIT barracks complex.

The buildings now had brass plaques that said *National Historic Site.* My building had a fresh coat of paint, looking like it was built yesterday and so true to its original it could have been a movie set. I remembered thundering down those front steps and falling into formation in the pre-dawn Oklahoma rain. I could see our fat sergeant standing on the dry porch while we stood shivering and waiting for permission to put on our ponchos.

The building was still in use. I walked through the front door and strolled up the center aisle. There was still a row of bunks down each side and I sought out my old spot, the third bunk from the end on the right. The shower room had not changed; it was still only a tiled room with nozzles positioned along the walls and a massive drain in the middle of the floor. The same latrine, with commodes in the open along the walls, conjured the chatter of guys sitting in a circle and discussing the day's events.

The building had been maintained in its historical form, but the place was a mess. The beds were half-made with blanket corners dragging on the floor. A litter of shoes, socks, combs, underwear, shampoo, deodorant and magazines surrounded the beds. As much as I had disliked the Army and its obsession with neatness, this was an insult to basic military discipline.

Upstairs I was shocked to find a pair of high heels under the first bed. This floor was worse than the one below. I thought, *Why do women need so many eye pencils, tubes of lipstick, hair dryers, curling irons and hand mirrors? And why in God's name can't they put them away?* I was now living with three women and perhaps too sensitive to the disarray that females seemed to find so comforting.

I paced around the building complaining about the modern Army. The barracks I had labored to keep meticulous was now a trash heap. I said to the air, "I would love to know who's in charge of this dump."

My daughters said in one voice, "Daaaaaaaaaad." They had a great deal of practice over the years in chanting this when I was in the act of embarrassing them, and now sang it with all the precision and emotion of a choir.

Walking out I stopped a staff sergeant, high enough in rank to be career military, and said, "Sergeant, that barracks is a disgrace."

Beautiful front teeth came out on his face and reminded me of Smoke, my old gun sergeant. This sergeant's teeth had no red heart and gold star, yet they held the same warmth and good humor. "Yes sir, those are reserve troops, only here on weekends. We pretty much leave them alone. Volunteer Army, you know."

I was about to say, "That's no excuse," when I felt the look of three females drilling into the back of my neck. I said, "Sergeant, can you tell me how to get to the PX?" No matter where women go, they are compelled to shop, and the Post Exchange seemed a good way to make peace.

The sergeant turned to the street in front of the barracks. He pointed to the left and said, "It's four blocks to the right; can't miss it."

I smiled to myself that some of the Old Army still survived in this kindly man. I said, "Thanks, Sarge. Good luck with the amateurs."

Before embarking on our search for the PX, there was a last thing that needed doing. I led us to a spot outside the barracks where a set of chin-up bars used to stand. That piece of ground had grown sacred in my memory. On the clear night of July 21, 1969, I looked up in wonder at the moon, where Neil Armstrong, Michael Collins and Buzz Aldrin had landed the day before.

I said, "I stood on this very spot when man first landed on the moon. Imagine that: people walking around on another planet."

Ellen produced a loud sigh. Elizabeth raised her eyes to me and said, "Can we go now?"

Today, none of the old barracks remain. All were torn down or sold off to make room for more brick buildings the size of warehouses. One barracks went to a group that took it away and turned it into a church.

The Memorial

There is no war memorial like it in the world, and I did not want to see it. On periodic business trips to Washington I had plenty of opportunities. But when my traveling companions suggested a trip to the Vietnam Memorial I always let them go without me. They never pressed for a reason; I could not have given them one if they had.

I was certain that a fear of reliving a trauma was not what held me back. I had an easy go of it compared to the average rifleman slogging through the jungles and rice paddies. Since returning from Vietnam twenty years earlier I had not had a single dream about it. I had no real conflicts about serving in Vietnam, no moral compunction or any strong sentiment that ran counter to my actions. Once I learned the rules, both official and unspoken, and figured out how to navigate the maze of nonsense and contradictions that defined the U.S. Army in those days, I was a pretty happy fellow. Sure, I hated being in the military, nothing new there, but I was not torn up inside like some guys. Through good luck I was spared the horrors of direct fighting with the NVA and VC. Like everyone at LZ

Sherry I endured the mortar and rocket attacks, and lived with the possibility that we could be overrun at any time, but in the end my combat experiences were mild.

Maybe I did not want to see the grief of children and spouses. I did not know. The images on television were hard enough to watch. People holding one another by the shoulders and crying. Tortured souls pressing their hands to the etched names of departed sons, daughters, husbands and mothers, most of them just kids at the time, last seen alive when they shipped out, bravely telling everyone not to worry. Now gone forever, next met at Langley in a coffin. No chance to say a final goodbye, to hold a hand or kiss a forehead not yet cold. Piles of flowers against the granite and against personal walls of sorrow. People making rubbings of a name, a poor resurrection but something special to possess. The rangers putting ladders against the wall to reach names the chronology of death had lifted out of reach. Protesters laying Purple Hearts and other medals against the wall in repudiation of the war, or in honor of the fallen: no one knew the motivation, so conflicted were the times.

Perhaps I was afraid of the strange power of the place to stir emotions, when I had not yet figured out my own. It was only two granite walls embedded in the earth with a list of names chiseled into its surface. Visitors saw the names of every individual killed or missing in Vietnam, listed according to the date of death. In its polished surface, by a small adjustment of the eyes, they saw their own image standing in common with the dead. There were no statues to inspect, no inscriptions to read, no tree-lined vistas, no distractions to hide the raw truth.

What kind of person could conceive of such a memorial?

The design was chosen by a blind competition among 1,421 submissions. A panel of eight architects and sculptors unanimously chose entry number 1026. The winner turned out to be Maya Ying Lin, a twenty-one-year-old undergraduate student at Yale and first generation Chinese American from Athens, Ohio.

Few people outside the committee were happy with the design. Veterans called it a black gash of shame. Two early supporters of the project, Ross Perot and James Webb, withdrew their endorsements. Webb, a Vietnam veteran, said, "I never in my wildest dreams imagined such a nihilistic slab of stone." Perot called Maya Lin an "egg roll" when he learned she was Asian. James Watt, Secretary of the Interior, refused to issue a building permit. Maya Lin, not long out of her teenage years, went before Congress to explain her design, an act of bravery that deserved its own memorial.

Eventually a compromise was reached. Another memorial would also be built, a single statue depicting in realistic detail three infantrymen outfitted in combat uniforms and equipment. When Maya Lin learned the stature was to stand beside her wall she was outraged, and soon succeeded in getting it moved some distance away.

Before the statue could be installed, Maya Lin's wall had already captured the heart of the American people. Veterans in worn fatigues were seen leaning against the wall with their hands on a buddy's name and weeping. They were also seen at the statue, but there debating over an ammo belt or commenting on the details of a flak jacket.

How could a young girl, with no experience of what the Vietnam veteran had endured, get it so right? Jan Scruggs offers the best explanation. He is a wounded Vietnam veteran who came up with the idea of the memorial in 1979 and became the

Vietnam Veterans Memorial President. "It has helped people separate the warrior from the war, and it has helped a nation to heal. It has become something of a shrine."

Maya Lin did not need to know anything about battles or military equipment. Instead she exposed to the sunlight America's invisible scar.

My manager of corporate recruitment and I were in Washington to visit headhunter firms. He suggested we eat up a few hours of free time with a trip to the memorial.

I said, "Alright. This will be my first visit."

"First time? Are you OK with this?"

"Sure, why wouldn't I be?"

Outside the memorial there were kiosks holding a thick book. It listed the names on the wall in alphabetical order, followed by the panel on which the name was located. I opened one of the books, and without thinking flipped to the G's to make sure my name was not there. I felt something within me, a small weight, slip into place and find a resting spot. To this day I cannot put the right words to what happened within me. The closest I can come is: *A lot of people died but I didn't. I could have a couple times, but didn't. And it's OK.* I simmered in that warm moment for a long time, the whole while pretending to study the book.

When the feeling cooled I looked up and found my companion. I said, "Let's get going and see what this thing is all about. We haven't got all day you know."

Never Too Late

I was sitting in the bar at a reunion of the 27th Field Artillery with Andy Kach and Henry Parker, both of whom had been at LZ Sherry the year before me. Henry Parker was the battery commander, and Andy was assigned to the ammo section but sometimes fired the howitzers when they were shorthanded. Andy began telling the story of the ground attack at LZ Sherry, the one that occurred the year before I arrived and which I had heard a little about when I first arrived.

Andy said, "I'll never forget that ground attack. Thank God we caught them in the wire. I spent the next day picking body parts out of the concertina. There was a piece we called 'Head and Shoulders' because that was all that was left of him. Turned out to be our Vietnamese barber." With a crooked smile he said, "They brought lunch out to me, and when I sat down to eat I looked over and saw a leg next to me. I suddenly lost my appetite."

Captain Parker said, "It was a bloody year. The NVA hit us every day, sometimes two and three times. And they were damn good. Why they could drop a mortar in a bushel basket.

In a three-month stretch I went from 116 men to forty-eight. Not every wounded guy went to the rear. If he could still walk and shoot, he stayed."

"Like me," Andy said. "I get blown out of the guard tower and mess up the side of my head. Four days later my face is so swollen I can't eat and stuff is leaking out of my ear. I finally say maybe I should go to the rear and have it looked at."

Parker said, "You should have told me sooner. I still feel guilty."

"If you had known," Andy said, "would you have let me go?"

Parker laughed. "Probably not."

Andy said, "At the hospital in Phan Rang they pull six of my teeth and put me on antibiotics. In two weeks I'm back at Sherry. One day I'm on a work detail out on the perimeter when a guy comes out and tells me to get my shirt and hat and report to the battery commander. They give me a Purple Heart and ten minutes later I'm back out shoveling sand again. Purple Hearts were nothing special. That's why when a guy was going to Sherry they'd ask him what's his favorite shade of purple."

The captain turned in my direction. "Andy's getting another medal tomorrow at the banquet, long overdue. He was getting ready for the reunion and checking his discharge papers to make sure he had all the right ribbons for his uniform, which he still had and wanted to wear to the banquet. He saw the letters BSM tacked onto the abbreviation for the Vietnamese service ribbon. So he calls me up and says, 'What does BSM stand for?' I tell him it stands for Bronze Star Medal. He says, 'No, I didn't get a Bronze Star, it must stand for something else.' I tell him, 'Andy, you got a Bronze Star whether you knew it or not. Hell, they gave me a Silver Star along with a Bronze Star for valor and I didn't know it for years.' I tell him I'll track it down, and I did. It wasn't hard."

At the Friday banquet a table sat off to the side with an empty chair and place setting, a reminder never to forget fallen comrades. Sergeant Dave Fitchpatrick read the names of the forty-eight men of the regiment who had died in combat, seven of them in just one year at LZ Sherry. Hank and Andy folded a ritual flag into a triangle and placed it on a side table. Captain Parker walked to the head of the room and called for Specialist 4 Andrew Kach to step forward. Forty-one years after leaving Vietnam, Andy stood at attention as Captain Parker read the citation from the Department of the Army awarding him the Bronze Star Medal with "V" device for valor. Then his old battery commander pinned the medal on Andy's chest next to his Purple Heart.

Two Old Soldiers

Curly, the section chief I had helped displace in FDC, was at the reunion. To my relief he did not remember our early difficulties, which allowed me to put that ghost to rest. But he still lived with the memory of his dismissal from officer school; it burned like a hot coal the years could not cool. He retold the story with as much pain as I remembered it from our conversations over the cribbage board in Vietnam.

I said, "You told me once you thought the Army did you a favor."

He said, "Well, it saved me ten months in the military." This was as much peace as he was able to bring to the memories.

Curly and I made a special trip to the Ft. Sill artillery museum with Kathleen in tow. Immediately inside the door was a revolutionary war cannon and a plaque about Henry Knox, the father of American artillery. Curly and I walked through the decades of artillery technology and were struck by how little our howitzers at LZ Sherry had changed from WWII. Around a corner we came by surprise upon that Fucking Freddie FA-

DAC, a barely functioning computer we were forced to use in 1970. We both groaned.

As we were leaving the museum I peeked around a corner and saw a small display case on the wall. It contained a complete set of fire direction instruments, looking as if they had come directly from our FDC bunker at LZ Sherry. There was a map like the one on which we had plotted so many fire missions and nighttime positions. There was the little square plotting scale for getting grid coordinates precisely correct. There was the range deflection protractor we used to determine direction and distance to the target, and the graphical slide rules for computing firing data. There was the round target grid we used when the forward observer adjusted smoke and moved artillery shells around the target.

These paper, wood and metal things were once so alive in our hands. Looking at them now brought back the mortar attacks and the fire missions. I could almost hear the radio calls from a forward observer shouting into his handset, the howitzers blasting and the clatter of machine guns. Was that gunpowder I smelled?

The crowds of young people walking by only glanced. The little case was unremarkable among the more dramatic cannons, howitzers and displays of snappy 18th century uniforms. It said nothing to them, just as the WWI field gun I had touched could tell nothing of the carnage it had seen. Curly and I, two museum pieces ourselves, continued out of the building and into the sunlight.

The Lucky Ones

For thirty-five years I did not have a single dream about Vietnam, nor did I suffer from flashbacks or other difficulties connected to Vietnam. I always put my good fortune down to the fact that I had no moral conflicts about the war. Once I learned to navigate the nonsense and contradictions that defined the US Army in those days, I was a pretty happy fellow. Sure, I despised the military, nothing new there, but I was not torn up inside like some guys.

One night without warning I found myself back in the Army, at a facility too much like basic training at Ft. Leonard Wood, and on my way to Vietnam again. I said to anyone who would listen, "I've already been in for two years. I been to Vietnam. This is a big mistake."

A sergeant said, "Doesn't matter. New policy."

I woke up with a pounding heart and glad to be in the real world. The dream never returned, but proved that I did return from Vietnam with a small piece of baggage: the fear that I would have to do it all over again.

Beyond this silly dream, I have experienced none of the

torment suffered by so many men who served at LZ Sherry before me. Add up my combat experiences—mortar and rocket attacks, a little sniper fire here and there, the constant possibility of a ground assault, countless fire missions, the infantry guys on the radio in desperate situations, the body counts sometimes including our guys—and they do not come to much compared to the majority of men who served in the field.

 I was exposed to Agent Orange from it being sprayed around the perimeter to keep down the weeds. Before I arrived a team of guys sprayed 110 gallons of it undiluted around the wire—equivalent to over a thousand gallons. Yet so far I have escaped the host of ailments the military now acknowledges are created by exposure to Agent Orange, from cancer to diabetes.

I never talk about Vietnam without saying, "I'm one of the lucky ones."

THE LONG ARM
OF VIETNAM

When we came out of that war we may still have been young, but we were wise beyond our years.

-General Anthony C. Zinni
Commander In Chief, U.S. Central Command

It Don't Mean Nothin'

Maybe not at the time, but afterward Vietnam meant a lot to all of us. Every minute of it. No matter how long ago we served, we live with it in some fashion. Vietnam has a long arm, its hand always on our shoulder. On some it rests heavily, reminding us of things we would like to forget but cannot. Or it recalls exciting times, the tales growing more colorful with each telling, making us heroes in our own stories. For the lucky ones like me, that year was a training ground for later life. But Vietnam did more than broaden my perspective. It added fire to my convictions, because the lessons learned in combat are never held lightly.

Leadership

In Vietnam I served under great leaders, as well as the incompetent and comically out of touch. In a funny twist I learned as much from the bad leaders as I did from the good. I saw that every good leader put his men first, every bad one his career. The memory of Captain Crazy standing on the berm looking through his binoculars even today makes me angry. Then I remember Top, Lt. Christenson, Smoke, Junk Daddy, Lt. Rudewieck, Captain Joe and even Swede. All had a creative disrespect for the rigidities of Army and cared deeply about the boys in their charge.

The good leaders knew which orders to ignore, which to follow partially, which to slow walk and which to reinterpret, knowing that the underground carried on the real business of the military. They depended on the skill of soldiers who operated through handshake understandings and shadowy deals.

Under the assumption that little in the Army was as it appeared, the good leaders tolerated violations so long as they were camouflaged. Captain Joe and the rest of the leadership at LZ Sherry knew we stockpiled artillery rounds we never shot.

All of them had a hand in the internment of the tools caper. None of them cared that I invented information on maintenance forms, provided the paperwork went in on time and the oil in the jeeps really got changed.

These and a hundred other misdemeanors taught me that every organization needs a certain amount of healthy deception in order to function. By the time I entered the corporate world I knew to tell my subordinates *what* needed doing, not *how* to do it. I said, "Just stay out of jail."

I came away from Vietnam with a simple approach to leadership. *People come first.* In my corporate career I have counseled hundreds of junior leaders. I said to all of them, in different words over the years, "Take care of your people and they will take care of the business. Your career will take care of itself."

Fear

Everyone was afraid in Vietnam, all the time. We just had different ways of showing it.

On my first morning at LZ Sherry, at the mere sound of an AK47 aimed in my direction, I forgot my upbringing and overthrew years of priestly formation. In a blink I was ready to kill. It was oh-so easy, no more bother than lifting a finger. Later I cowered behind a flak wall, as helpless as a bug on a pin, knowing the explosions were my own howitzers, but frozen in a false belief that enemy mortars were still falling and that one of them was meant for me. After a time I grew tired of being afraid. Instead I pretended to be immortal, and just to prove it tried to run around with the infantry as a forward observer. My excuse at the time was that I was bored.

Reflecting years later on just how frightened I was that whole year, I have come to appreciate not so much the raw power of fear so much as its subtlety. In its various forms it pushed me to abandon personal values; it created beliefs that trumped the evidence of my senses; and in the end it robbed me of basic common sense.

As I matured in my corporate career I grew into a kind of coach to other leaders who were struggling or deeply unhappy. Most often I saw they abused their employees and distrusted fellow workers not because they were stupid or cruel, but out of hidden fears.

Often I heard something like, "If only Marketing would do its job I would not have all these problems."

I would say, "What are you afraid is going to happen?"

Then it came pouring out: a Technicolor movie of the catastrophe to come—poor advertising, a subsequent loss of promotion dollars, plummeting sales, a ruined career, children forced on the street to beg…theme music…fade to black…roll credits. Before long we would be laughing at the monster under the bed that turned out to be a dust ball. Now the conversation could focus on what was real: market test results, the option to shift dollars to point-of-sale advertising which might be better in the southern region anyway. Free of the grip of fear, the executive could think creatively and have a productive conversation with Marketing.

Was it this easy every time? Of course not. Sometimes I had to dig, because I knew, just *knew* a deep seated fear had made a nest in the center of this person's difficulties. Vietnam taught me to shovel it out like going after a rat hiding in its hole.

The Tyranny of Names

When I got my first body count at LZ Sherry I reacted like most guys. I thought of the sons, fathers and brothers I had killed. Their families haunted me. Then in imitation of the veterans I began calling them *gooks*. In that simple act my scruples vanished. Now I had a name for the enemy to erase all doubt about my job. Gooks were little more than animals. Hunting and killing them became almost a sport. The name justified anything. When fueled by fear, its power was virtually invincible. I went swiftly to the role of cold killer because I had no place else to run.

There is no equal in human language to the power of a name. It sets a filter that lets through only what is consistent with the name; we see and hear only what it will allow. Label an average child as *slow*, and even the best teachers will quite unconsciously treat the child in ways that reinforce the label. Politicians know that half the battle of winning an election is getting a name to stick to an opponent.

Early in my career at Anheuser-Busch I witnessed a dedicated employee acquire the label *stubborn*. He was passionate and perhaps too blunt for his own good. At the same time he understood his markets better than his bosses and was worth listening to.

Once the label stuck it defined the whole person and dictated how his bosses treated him. They grew deaf to everything he had to say. They focused on his manner and ignored the content. They moved him from boss to boss, job to job, at every move marginalizing him just a little more.

When he finally awoke to the ruined state of his career, he made attempts to change. He softened his tone, he chose his words more carefully, and he billed himself as a team player. To no avail, for the label by then was so in control that others read *obstruction* in the twitch of a facial expression and heard *disagreement* in the inflection at the end of a sentence. No matter what he did to change perceptions, he was forever preserved in amber as the stubborn employee.

It was a double tragedy. He suffered under a label he could not shake, and management lost the expertise of an employee who had a great deal to offer.

Like fears, labels thrive when they go unexamined. And like fears, they can be surprisingly easy to expose. When talking to managers I keep an ear out for the casually uttered label and try to catch it in the open, like nailing a rabbit running between bushes.

Here is an invented dialog, but representative of many I have had with managers about their employees.

Executive: "Harriet is an introvert and I'm not sure she's suited for the next level."

 Me: "Introvert. What makes you say that?"

"Well, she's quiet; doesn't talk much."

"Can you give me an example?"

"Sure, at meetings she's always the last one to say something. I notice stuff like that. I think it says something."

"Is it good stuff…when she finally decides to weigh in?"

"Oh, of course. I didn't say she was stupid."

"And do people listen to her?"

"Well, yeah. She knows her stuff."

Me: "Hmmm." …always a good line.

Executive, after a pause: "So it doesn't matter if she's an introvert? She's got all these other qualities, a hidden jewel kind of thing?"

"I don't know, but why not go with *hidden jewel* for a while and see where that leads. She might surprise you."

Unplugged

A picture of the abandoned guard tower that became my special place of refuge from the stresses of Vietnam hangs on the wall above my desk. The tower rises on sturdy legs above a sea of barbed wire, silhouetted black against a violet sunrise. It is the only memento of Vietnam I see every day, and the only picture of Vietnam I never tire of.

Over the years I have thought back to the insight about Curly that came to me in the tower: *Show him that you like him.* It was such an unlikely thing to pop into my mind, one I would never have come to on my own.

That was the start of figuring out that letting go a little, not trying so hard, leaves room for the world to come around on its own terms. The part of our brain that works on math problems and builds bridges is just a thin sliver of our full capability. Yet it wants to be in charge of everything, always giving instructions and whispering, *Do this* and *Don't do that.*

Unplugging this little dictator can work miracles. Conflicts somehow soften. I laugh more. Fewer surprises bother me. I worry less. I start to accept things for the way they are, instead of agitating for how I want them to be. Insights come of their own accord. A better *me* emerges I did not know was there, and I find myself wondering, *Is life supposed to be this easy?*

Three Questions

I was surprised when my effort worked so well to get Curly to believe I liked him, when I could hardly stand being in the same bunker with him. We shortly became genuine friends. But why did it work? For years I felt an intellectual itch to fill in the rest of the picture.

While at Anheuser-Busch I came by a thin book that gave a compelling explanation. When we meet a person for the first time—Curly for example—that person has three questions in mind that need to be answered for the relationship to proceed. These questions are usually not explicit, the person typically is not even aware of them. Nonetheless they are universally present in one form or another. The questions need to be answered in strict order: answering the second before the first will not do, nor answering the third before the second.

These are the questions I wish I had known were behind my early dealings with Curly. Perhaps I would not have made such a fool of myself.

1. Are you going to hurt me?
2. Do you care about me?

3. What do you want me to do?

In my ignorance and haste to take control I skipped over answering the first two questions. Instead I raced ahead to giving orders when Curly was still working on an answer to the first question, *Are you going to hurt me?* The answer I am sure he heard from me was, *Yes indeed.*

Over my corporate career I watched a parade of executives march into new assignments and get it exactly backwards, just as I did. They arrive giving orders, questioning every decision of their subordinates, and making silly announcements such as, *I'm here to get results.* The more energetic of the bunch start getting rid of veterans and hiring new experts, under the banner of upgrading the talent. One executive even said to her new department, "You've got to earn my trust." She little realized it was the other way around. It is no wonder that when such an executive assumes command the good people leave at the earliest opportunity; and those that stay spend their time digging foxholes.

What a difference it makes when a new leader comes at the job from the opposite direction. There are no grand reorganizations or dramatic announcements, which sends the message, *I am not a threat.* She listens intently and asks follow-up questions. *Not only am I not going to hurt you, I like you and care about what you think.* Now she has a foundation for rallying the team to action. *Let's talk about what we need to get done.*

The most important word in that last sentence is: *we.* There is nothing so powerful in all of human nature as a cohesive team. It must be the first priority of a new boss. Sure, there are people who do not fit their jobs and eventually need to be moved, but this is infinitely less important than the team. In fact attempting to fix individual personnel problems as a first priority tells the group, *I am in the process of hurting people, and you might be next.* The boss who believes there is no time for such niceties, especially if there is a crisis to address, will soon discover that it takes two years to repair a department paralyzed by suspicion and silent resentment, while it only requires a month or two to first build a trusting relationship with the group.

A classic leadership framework says that an effective executive must excel in the two dimensions of People and Task. The new leader would be wise to write four words on a piece of paper and paste it on the mirror at home so that at the beginning of every day it serves as a reminder. The note should remain for two months, at which time it can be thrown away. It should read:

PEOPLE FIRST
THEN TASK

I would like to give credit to the author of the book containing the three questions, but I cannot remember either the title of the book or the author's name.

It Helps to be a
Little Crazy

In Vietnam it was always the other guy who was crazy.

The people in the rear thought the guys in the field were nuts because they lied, cheated, pilfered as a way of life, and in the depths of their depravity had no respect for rank. The guys in the field thought the rear was utterly insane, perfectly and blissfully disconnected from reality. Both were right from the perspective of their worlds. One was a world of artillery shells and the other piles of paper, each with its rules of survival.

The major who vacationed from the rear by spending a night at LZ Sherry went from numbers jockey to warrior in a single night shift. Though a little rattled he was keen to fire off the artillery shells he so jealously counted the day before. Two days after leaving us he was back to hassling us about ammunition, and by our standards was again unhinged. From his perspective he had simply returned to behaving according to the world in which he had to function. His rank of major made it even more compelling to conform, and to by-God execute the job with gusto.

Unlike the visiting major, Captain Crazy did not have the

ability to adapt. He enforced the regulations too literally in a field operation where they often had no relevance. Once the *crazy* label stuck the troops saw only odd behavior, even when he played the game to near perfection, such as his orchestration of the visit of the Secretary of the Army.

The person who gives up a lucrative career in the corporate world to be a high school teacher—is he delusional? The young woman who gives up husband, children and a family to become a nun in the inner city—is she playing with a full deck? The surgeon who works only for money and cares little for her patients—an obsessive-compulsive narcissist? No, they are all perfectly sane within the world they have chosen to inhabit. Let them be. They have chosen the life that makes the most sense to them and which lights in them a special passion, as crazy as it may seem.

To Bear or Not to Bear Arms

I love guns. They are mechanically fascinating things and I never grew tired of firing them. I was proficient or minimally capable of handling the .45 pistol, M14 rifle, M16 rifle, M79 grenade launcher and both the M60 and .50-caliber machine guns.

Learning how to load, fire and clean these weapons was easy. It was infinitely more difficult using them during the chaos of combat—when lives hung in the balance, when all was confusion, bright flashes and deafening noise, when fear had a grip on one's innards. That took cold composure, which did not come with the instruction manual or practice on a firing range. It came only one way: through experience, which unfortunately required being shot at.

Soldiers in the combat specialties went to Vietnam with intensive training in the use of firearms. They were perhaps the best trained and equipped soldiers in history. Yet many turned irrational and unpredictable under live fire. That was the reason we were not issued weapons at LZ Sherry until we had been through a mortar attack. We first had to get control of ourselves before we could be trusted with a deadly weapon.

Even then the emotions of the moment could be overwhelming. A highly trained but frightened soldier almost shot a comrade during an attack on LZ Sherry. I myself, even after months in Vietnam, cowered behind a flak wall when I knew the real danger had passed. I was certainly in no condition to use my weapon. The memory still disturbs me, mostly because I have no explanation for why I panicked; I just did.

I came home believing that a person who has never experienced the exchange of real gunfire, no matter how well instructed, is more a danger to himself and others than to a bad guy, or worse to an imagined bad guy. I will remember forever looking down the barrel of a .357 magnum in the hands of a shaken golf course caretaker.

I know the thrill of holding a gun. The solid weight and comfortable balance give a rush of power. Practice leads to greater proficiency and speed in operation, creating an even greater sense of mastery. Knowing the gun is close at hand completes the sense of having control over any situation. I know from experience that these feelings are illusions, wrapped in imagination, based on fantasy. We fantasize about confronting the bad guy; we imagine ourselves to be powerful with a weapon in our hands, the great equalizer; we dwell within the illusion that now we are safe and capable of defending ourselves. I harbored all of these romantic notions. But they are a thin gauze that can melt away when a shadow passes the bedroom door, surely a burglar or rapist. They disappear in an instant in the midst of a public shooting, where confusion and panic are akin to a combat situation. We act without thinking and suddenly—we never remember quite how it happened—a bleeding body lies on the ground. Now we are liable for our actions.

Does the body belong to the bad guy, or some other law abiding citizen who had also drawn his weapon, or perhaps to an innocent bystander?

Guns are the only products in our society that are designed to kill. Yet most guns, to include military style assault weapons, are owned by amateurs, people with no personal experience in the use of deadly force. We would not think of asking an accountant to remove an appendix. What then causes us to believe this accountant is capable of a proper killing with the handgun he got for Christmas? Holstering a loaded gun in the morning as routinely as slipping on a wrist watch is not the path to a safe society.

Even with all of my training and combat experience, I no longer have the coolness and presence of mind to pull a gun on another person. Even so, I did not leave Vietnam to recreate it here at home. I choose not to carry a gun into society or to keep one in my home. I have put aside the image of a gun as a trusted friend, and instead think of it as a grenade with the pin pulled, ready to kill with the mere move of a finger.

War

"Don't you boys know that violence never solved anything?"

When Top pulled the fighting boys apart in the middle of a combat zone with those words, I began asking myself a question. If violence cannot resolve problems between just two people, what leads us to believe it will work any better between two nations?

The reason is simple. From our experience we know that when two people go at each other with rifles, knives, fists, baseball bats, rocks, spears, dueling pistols, sharpened pencils or golf clubs, nothing is ever resolved. It does not require logic to convince us of this because we have all experienced it as true.

In the business of armed conflict between nations, the people who make the war have rarely experienced its devastation, or felt the terror of combat.

In the lead-up to the armed conflicts the United States has entered since Vietnam, the public figures who had served in WWII, Korea or Vietnam were the most reluctant to go to war again. Yet how often were these patriots, these war heroes, these men and women who risked their lives in service to their country, how many times were they accused of disloyalty or of appeasing the enemy—by people who lived comic book lives, who had no notion of the realities of war, who puffed themselves up with rhetoric about national honor, who demonized their opponent with false analogies and half-truths?

It is difficult to fully appreciate the carnage of Vietnam. Most know that more than 58,000 U.S. soldiers died. We honor them down to the individual with their names etched on a polished granite wall. Few realize that another 304,704 were wounded, 153,303 seriously enough to be hospitalized, leaving many with devastating disabilities.

Even fewer of us know, or perhaps care, that close to three million Vietnamese lost their lives in that conflict. The numbers are so large and indefinite that they are rounded to the nearest thousand. The South Vietnamese Army lost 266,000, half of them killed in the two years between the U.S. withdrawal in 1973 and the fall of Saigon in 1975. Despite my first negative impressions of ARVN forces, they fought valiantly and showed a willingness to die for their country. Some believe they were more committed to the fighting than U.S. forces.

The NVA and VC combined lost 1,100,000. Every year 10,000 died of disease: yellow fever, malaria, dengue fever, the black plague and cholera. Civilian deaths totaled 843,000 during the war. Another 643,000 civilians died as the North Vietnamese consolidated power.

I made my small contribution to these numbers. My job in Vietnam was to kill gooks, and I was good at it. But today they aren't gooks in my mind. They are fathers, husbands and children. Like me they had families, friends and ambitions outside of warfare. Sometimes I think about them. And I think of

Slick, Wan, Cindy and Mama-san. Did they flee the advancing NVA, perhaps perishing with 100,000 other civilians? Did they end up in re-education and labor camps, where 320,000 civilians died? Or were they executed along with 200,000 people accused of collaborating with the enemy?

Of the many pictures I brought back from Vietnam, one grabs my heart in a special way. It shows a boy, perhaps nineteen years of age and hardly shaving, doing his laundry from a metal ammunition can. The can sits on a stack of artillery ammo boxes next to a crumbled box of Cold Power. Sandbags and more artillery boxes form the walls of the little laundry. The boy is standing in mud and wearing only his boxer shorts. A reach away just off the picture is his duty station: the four .50-caliber machine guns of *Murder Incorporated*.

The boy turns his head and lifts a dripping fatigue shirt. He could be saying, "Mom, I think I'll do my socks next." But he is a child at war, ready without pause to bring slaughter upon an enemy.

The picture reminds me that we were just kids, playing with deadly toys in a murderous game. But Vietnam was no different than any other war, or perhaps any war to come. Will that boy one day be my grandson or descendant yet unborn?

Casualty statistics are from: R.J. Rommel, *Vietnamese Democide: Estimates, Sources, and Calculations,* 1997; Osprey Warrior 135, *The North Vietnamese Army Soldier 1958-75.*

Friends and Enemies

Most friendships do not last. They are products of the situations in which they were born.

In Vietnam I thought I could never be closer to other human beings. I was ready to lay down my life for them, and they for me, yet today I cannot remember most of their names. I made an attempt to continue some of those friendships into civilian life when five of us got together in Florida. We talked for a few hours about Vietnam, laughed and kidded around. After that there was nothing more to talk about. One guy was going back to being a mechanic; another had bought a motorcycle and was going to bum around the country; I was off to graduate school. We shared only a past that was no more.

That was the beginning of my understanding that it is OK to let people go. New situations bring new friends. If I could get so close to someone in just a few months to be willing to die for him, the possibilities for making new friends must be limitless. Letting old friendships die opens a space and lets in the sunshine for new friendships to take root. It is nature's way.

Some friendships last, not because of the depth of emotional attachment, but because they are constantly renewed in the present. Kathleen and I had been married for eight years and just had Ellen, our second child, when in a moment of reflection I said to her, "You know, I think people stay married for very different reasons than they get married in the first place."

She shot me a look that only the Dark Irish can give, a look her father had, and said, "What do you mean by *that*?"

I heard the *thoomp* of an incoming mortar and headed for cover. Any attempt at explanation would not end well. I managed to say something like, "Just that I love you more today than ever."

I wanted to say that a wedding is only a brief moment in the flow of time. Things change so quickly that in a few years the young couple find themselves in entirely new circumstances. There is a mortgage, careers make enormous demands, dirty diapers need changing. The marriage will depend more on the division of labor for taking care of the kids, for example, than on the good times of past weekend ski trips. The staying power of any relationship depends on the *I-would-die-for-you* present.

If most friends are not forever, neither are enemies. At Anheuser-Busch I worked with a mild-mannered fellow with a charming Virginia accent. After I had known Cliff for about a year he told me of his time in Vietnam. He went into the jungle for weeks at a time, set up claymore mines along known VC routes, and tried to blow up as many of the enemy as he could. He did this for two tours of duty. Behind that gentle exterior and rounded diction there lived a very tough guy.

When the job opened to become the Anheuser-Busch sales representative to Vietnam, Cliff jumped at the chance. He told me the story of one 4th of July when he happened to be in Hanoi. He found himself sitting on a veranda with a retired Viet

Cong general, now a beer distributor. Fireworks in celebration of American independence lit the sky as they talked about the war.

The general said that the North prevailed because Americans came for only a year, while the Vietnamese fought until they died, were wounded or the war was over. "The Americans just wanted to go home," the general said. "We knew we could outlast them. We were willing to pay any price, while the Americans counted every casualty and put it in their newspapers."

Cliff said to me, "The general was right."

Then he showed a little southern smile and said, "I never imagined that one day I would be hoisting a Budweiser with a gook general. It was nice."

Ed Gaydos

Ed Gaydos and his wife of forty years, Kathleen, raised two daughters without major incident and now live in retired bliss in Columbus, Ohio.

Ed's debut book, *Seven in a Jeep: A Memoir of Vietnam*, is available from all major book retailers and as an e-book on all digital markets.

www.SeveninaJeep.com

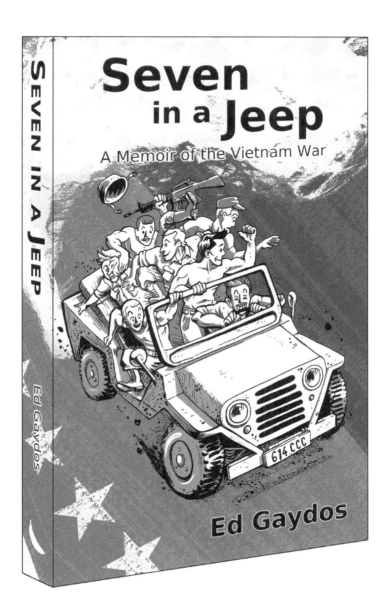

Seven
in a Jeep

A Memoir of the Vietnam War

Ed Gaydos

SEVEN IN A JEEP

Ed Gaydos

CPSIA information can be obtained
at www.ICGtesting.com
Printed in the USA
BVHW042032191222
654545BV00004B/456